What Others Are Saying . . .

Dr. Jacqueline Zaleski Mackenzie is, in my opinion, a truly courageous person. By having communicated with her I found a philanthropic, almost saint-like quality of her unselfishness, coupled with deep understanding and the desire to share her research. This book is recommended as an addition to all school libraries, and for course studies designed around this information for use as a text book. Anyone and everyone with an interest or curiosity in the Latino culture, and wishing to become aware of the emerging Spanish speaking majority, should seize the opportunity to buy this book and read it cover to cover. Real change will only occur through understanding, education, and having "our eyes wide open."

—GARY SORKIN,
Pacific Book Review

Dr. Mackenzie's study of Spanish/Latino children and the culture that affects their lives and their ability to learn is a compelling and informative work that allows greater understanding of the difficulties facing educators, not just those who teach Spanish/Latino children; but also those who work with any child from a multicultural background. *Empowering Spanish Speakers*, is definitely recommended by award-winning author and *Allbooks* reviewer,

—EMILY-JANE HILLS ORFORD,
Allbooks Reviews, www.allbooksreviewint.com

Empowering Spanish Speakers is the first book of its kind to identify the problems facing rural Latino families. It's a book that could change the lives of the millions of our Latino neighbors who are living 18th century lives while the rest of the world rapidly advances through the 21st century.

—CAROLE SCHOR,
Reviewer for the *San Miguel Literary Sala*

This kind of proximity allows her to reach conclusions not readily afforded to other researchers…*Empowering Spanish Speakers* covers all aspects the Mexican culture from childrearing to gender roles in the extended family and workplace. It includes a Q&A section, appendices of nutrition and developmental challenges for educators and caregivers, and a thorough works cited list. Although this book should be read straight through, Mackenzie adopts a standard how-to format. By using a series of symbols highlighting key areas regarding differences in learning styles, educators and business trainers will find this book invaluable for both detailed study and as a quick reference guide. And casual readers will discover new depths when savoring the literary traditions that gave the world Ignacio Padilla and Octavio Paz.

—JOSEPH THOMPSON,
Foreword Book Reviews

This is the best book I have ever read on the Mexican culture and I've read a lot of them.

—JON SEVERT,
Humble Press, San Miquel de Allende, Mexico

A guide to dealing with Spanish speaking individuals in many aspects of life, education, and business: Not everyone speaks English or can easily learn it, and it's best to understand that. *Empowering Spanish Speakers: Answers for Educators, Business People, and Friends of Latinos* is a guide to dealing with Spanish speaking individuals in many aspects of life, education, and business. From cultural differences that aren't entirely obvious and how this applies to teaching, reaching Spanish speaking marketing, and working with Spanish speakers in the business world. *Empowering Spanish Speakers* realizes there is more to communication than language and does well in filling readers into a more complete understanding across culture.

—*Midwest Book Review,*
Oregon, WI

This is a singular book. Well-researched data coupled with poignant personal experiences in the research field makes for a read that is captivating as well as informative. Written especially for teachers by a an educator motivated to make this critical information easily accessible, the format is engaging and utilitarian and therefore available for a wide ranging interest group. Most of all it is extremely timely given President Obama's recent speech regarding this very issue. Highly recommended.

—*Desert Teacher*

Tribute to a deeply researched and lived experience—Dr. Jacqueline Z. Mackenzie takes us into a live project that includes real kids in a rural setting and allows us to explore educational realities. We are brought face to face with the challenges that students face when placed in an environment where languages other than their own are used, not because the learner chose this situation. Unlike other places in the world where multilingualism is honored and rspected the US tends to consider this a tolerable problem and inconvenience. This book helps those who are and will be involved in the teaching process to recognize the connection between culture and language and its importance in the learning process. Maybe this book will help us turn this teaching process into a pleasurable exploration child's family and background . . .

—MIKE ROHRBACH,
SE Arizona based Information Literacy group implementing
Digital Libraries in rural Mexico

Mackenzie's program, "Speak with your heart" is her reply to teachers of Spanish speakers who say, "What should I do? I don't speak a word of Spanish." Sales of her book will be used to build libraries in rural Mexico. Sacrificing the comforts of western civilization to live in rural Mexico, Mackenzie's book is a guide to working with Spanish speaking persons from all walks of life. Her work combines scientific research, statistical analysis, and personal exploits in an easy-to-read textbook format.

—MIRIAM RODRÍGUEZ,
Assistant Director of Public Services, Dallas Public Library

Opposite: The indoor playroom is a daycare for infants to 5 years who are the children of people employed by the Mexican government. The facility will hold up to 450 children. Dr. Mackenzie volunteered there for two summers.

COMPANION GUIDE TO
*Empowering Spanish Speakers—Answers for Educators,
Business People, and Friends of Latinos*

Empowering
Teachers
of Latino
Children

A TOOLKIT FOR INSTRUCTING

SPANISH SPEAKERS—PRE-K

THROUGH MIDDLE SCHOOL

Dr. Jacqueline Zaleski Mackenzie

SUMMERLAND CORPORATION

Photos were used by permission. Edited by Carole Schor. Photos by Jacqueline Mackenzie. Artwork by Jolene Gailey. Cover and interior design by John Reinhardt Book Design. Symbols by Rob Oakes.

NOTE: Our publications reflect our opinions of what we have observed over a lifetime of living with Mexican-American immigrants and/or while living as residents in an impoverished, rural community in Central Mexico. We have recorded what we have learned with an academic's attention to detail to tell the whole story and improve comprehension by the reader. We may have made some incorrect assumptions about Mexican culture due to our own cultural biases; if so, we apologize to any people of the Mexican background whom we may have offended. Our nonprofit organization has published this information to help non-Mexicans to better comprehend Mexican culture.

Volunteers wrote and/or researched this book as an extension of the mission of our nonprofit 501©3 corporation, not as a public trade or business. Our publications are directly related to our exempt purpose: the education of disadvantaged Mexicans to reduce emigration from Mexico to the U.S. and the education of disadvantaged Mexican immigrants living in the U.S. We are offering these books for public viewing. Unquestionably, we have specifically directed our voices to the uninformed public teachers and corporate trainers of Spanish speakers who are Mexican nationals or Mexican immigrants. We would also like to welcome others, such as federal and state government officials, academic administrators, CEOs of corporations, foundation leaders, and school administrators, to read this book as well. We hope that what we have learned will help those working with any Mexican students anywhere. We hope, too, that this information will enable students to have an opportunity to earn an education that will facilitate self-sustainability.

We have priced the book for financial accessibility because we want to distribute it without undue hardship to the reader. We choose for the information to be widely and conveniently distributed to those we aim to serve; sale price covers the distribution expenses. Materials, computers, Internet access, and fees paid to print this book were donated to our nonprofit. Many people also donated their labor. All proceeds from the sale of this book will be used directly to allow our religious order to maintain our mission: the education of disadvantaged (predominately indigenous) Mexicans.

ISBN (print) 978-1-936425-04-4

ISBN (eBook) 978-1-936425-05-1

Published by: Summerland Corp. ATC aka Summerland Monastery, Inc. ATC
                2343 West Old Ajo Hwy
                Tucson, Arizona 85746-9113

Visit www.jacquelinemackenzie.com or www.spanishimmersioneducation.org for more information.

Printed in the United States of America.

This workbook is dedicated to educators of children. They are unselfish individuals who work under extreme pressure. Administrators give them unrelenting responsibility and minimal authority. Teachers give 65+ hours a week; they receive little compensation. Their experience, wisdom, and time make it possible for children to acquire literacy and other life skills.

Like a candle, they give of themselves
to light the way for others.

ACKNOWLEDGMENTS

Many thanks to those fellow publishers who helped me to reach a standard of quality equal to what the public regards as the highest available.

Many thanks to those who made certain this document met the highest standards of quality, including editor Carole Schor, cover and interior text designer John Reinhardt, proofreader Jolene Gailey, and original symbol designer Rob Oakes.

I would like to thank my husband, Donald James Mackenzie, and my soul sister Jolene Gailey for always overlooking my personal struggle for perfection.

Contents

PART THREE: Teacher's Guided Learning for Students

PART FOUR: Student Outcome

PART FIVE: Spanish Immersion—Each One Teach One

Symbols

The hand symbol stands for the traits of the student: What they ask, how they act, what interests them, etc. In Latin American countries, the student's school experience is typically confined to an indoor environment. The young person is usually shown abstract ideas that are taught using rote memory. He or she is given the answers to specific questions, and after memorizing the questions and the correct answers, the student is expected to answer assessments exactly as memorized. This process is completed without individual analysis and can even be completed without the understanding of the concepts. The training in youth establishes lifelong patterns.

The heart symbol stands for the instructor: What actions the teacher might take, or what types of lessons, modifications to the classroom environment, or other empowerment techniques he or she might implement to increase learning.

The plant symbol relates to the acquired knowledge of the student. He or she adds new information to the already acquired information, thereby building on the established foundation. This is the childhood pattern of learning in the outdoors, which results in enriched understanding and accelerated processing of information. This learning pattern is the result of being raised in outlying areas of Latin America. Outdoors, around family members of all ages, is where the rural Spanish speaking child actually learns and applies critical thinking skills. The child watches the elders and peers work, rarely speaking with them, and then he or she imitates the observed activities. The child applies individual analysis through trial and error, gaining understanding from personal failures and successes, and retaining what is learned.

Preface

This is a companion guide workbook, not a stand-alone manual. It is intended as a supplement to the textbook titled "Empowering Spanish Speakers—Answers for Educators, Business People, and Friends of Latinos." That textbook has complete footnotes, works cited, and a full index, this workbook does not; it is only a supplement. This book covers only the "How to" aspect of complex methods - quick and simple facts—you need in the classroom. After reading this you will have the tools to turn Latinos who are in pre-K to middle school into successful learners. In what manner you use these tools are entirely your choice.

To clarify—this book is only the "How" portion—about 160 "tips" that were the result of out of several complex cultural research projects. If you want the "who, what, when, where, and why," the footnotes for each reference, and complete list of works cited then refer to the original textbook: "Empowering Spanish Speakers—Answers for Educators, Business People, and Friends of Latinos."

Technology is breaking new ground. Today we live in a world that is moving faster, with less insight, and more access to knowledge than ever before. According to David "Skip" Prichard, President of the Ingram Books Company, this is an age when one New York Times holds more printed matter than a person born in the 1800's saw in a lifetime. Even experts have no idea what to call a book, a booklet, eBook, eReader, or some other yet to be created specific term All we know is that what you have in your hands is information recorded for your enlightenment and enjoyment.

Considering that unlike monks of an age past, this scribe is writing data on an electronic device that will be transferred first to paper. Where it will go after that is anyone's guess; a multitude of other options for assimilation exists. Options that today neither of us can imagine. All we know is that our future will be both diverse and integrated. Fortunately, how you gather what I have to say is irrelevant, but that you do with that information is paramount. As an informed teacher, you have always had the power to create either educated leaders of tomorrow or bored "seat-warmers," I call them.

I am deeply indebted to Latina women. For that reason, I am passionate about helping their children to be successful. Had I not felt such a commitment, I could have never written my first book. My own social marginalization is being a Polish immigrant's granddaughter and my author's disability is dyslexia. Nevertheless, with my hands on the keyboard and a great deal of fear of failure, I listened to the words of Eleanor Roosevelt:

We gain strength, and courage, and confidence by each experience in which we really stop to look fear in the face...we must do that which we think we cannot.

PART ONE

Self-Evaluation

1

Attitude is the Key

Attitudes are contagious. Are yours worth catching?

—Dennis and Wendy Mannering

The only disability in life is a bad attitude.

—Scott Hamilton

Justification

Every teacher possesses the power to bring a student out of the darkness of ignorance and into the light of knowledge. Conversely, that power can also transform a lighthearted, eager student into a broken child wallowing in despair with permeating fear of anything associated with school.

Understand Your Influence

Teachers and parents play the primary role in influencing tomorrow's Latino leaders. I totally agree with other researchers who make the statement that **students make up their minds by age 11 or 12 whether education and academics are worthwhile pursuits**. And having made that decision, the student drops out mentally (becoming only a "seat-warmer"), if not physically, when the opportunity presents itself. *That concept makes pre-K to middle school the most important years in the life of a person* and therefore, you the most important person in their life while they are being influenced by you.

Consider your passions, strengths and weaknesses. Ask yourself if you are capable of being a social justice advocate for Latinos.

- Are you willing to provide a supportive environment that is socioculturally appropriate for your Spanish speaking students?
- Are you committed to creating a stimulating space that is a continuous stream of activities designed specifically to enhance linguistic, cognitive, academic, and social development?
- Will you demand quality work or expect less from Latinos?

Inventory

This book is based on a variety of sources, including my observations, research, interviews, and group meetings, as well as extensive study of publications by other authors, academic, and otherwise. Take what works and use it; ignore what doesn't work in your situation.

Keep in mind that an article titled *Experts Call for Early Focus on Black Boys' Nonacadmeic Skills* by Mary Ann Zejer on June 15, 2011 stated:

> "…the Princeton, N.J.-based Educational Testing Service and the Washington-based Children's Defense Fund also said that a significant portion of the dollars spent on incarcerating black males in this country would be better spent on high-quality early-childhood education."

Your efforts, for children of color, are always highly necessary even if no one remembers to tell you that fact. In the same way that you know taking all those pedagogy and methods classes left a wasteland of unexplored questions, do not ever think that a day or two of "in-service" meetings at the beginning of the school year has prepared you for the tough job ahead with a diverse population.

First Step: Know more about yourself –

Examine yourself like you were standing in front of a mirror. Then step back and look even deeper at your:

1. emotions
2. passions
3. social status
4. overall outlook

Then do a personal evaluation—write down what you identify.

Personal Inventory Template

This can be a narrative (like I did below), a drawing like mind mapping, an outline, a video, verbal record that is taped—choose any format, just do it.

Most days I cannot imagine that I am any older than 35 years of age. I feel youthful, strong, mentally alert, tall, and capable of doing anything I can imagine. When the pain of my aging joints slows my progress, I'm annoyed because I have cared for my health with the precision and determination of a trained surgeon since high school. The will power I have shown, related to health issues, I have never known in anyone else I knew personally. Like assignments in a course syllabus, I've spent 48 years of my life reading publishers of health articles, cookbook related to health, anti-aging guides, exercise books, yoga, psychology, natural beauty and other health related self-help materials. However, I do not resist aging; I resist illness. I love being "grandma to 100" as I call myself, but slowing down is simply not acceptable.

Falling off my feisty, brazen, athletic four-year-old mare really upsets my view of myself as a cowgirl of some skill. I don't claim to be accomplished, but I do claim to be experienced and agile enough to ride and control her. Apparently, I'm not able to help her overcome her "spookiness."

What has remained constant in my life is a burning desire to know for myself the truth. What I mean is the truth about anything, the absolute, wide, definitive, complete truth. "How to" is my middle name.

My passion for knowing all is what drove me to move to a small native community of subsistence farmers in the high mountains of Central Mexico. For several years, I was a teacher of special needs students who were Spanish speakers. I was not able to reach them like I felt I should be able to do. I was not sure why. I was certain the answers were out there someplace. I read every book, in English, that I could find written by native Spanish speakers who had left their homeland. I got some answers, but not enough answers. Because I am a non-conformist and adore research, I went looking myself.

One clear example of what I found: I recall watching my first class of middle school student boys take an attitude of having "finished" all formal schooling at the end of middle school. Until I moved to Mexico and realized that most of the men in the village *had finished their formal schooling by fifth grade or earlier*. I also learned that most houses had no printed matter, there were no rural libraries, there were no such things as on-going adult education programs; in summary formal studies took a back seat to basic human survival. Apparently, that mindset was so deeply engrained that the first generation or two in the USA did not modify their outlook. I am now questioning if those who often visit rural Latin America, as a result of making comparisons with native relatives living in rural environments, simply reinforce old habit patterns of not anticipating attending high school or higher education programs as a necessity for adult occupations.

Second Step: Know more about the people you are influencing—

Educators or instructors who are well informed and sensitive can accomplish miracles. In the words of Dr. Wayne Dyer, "Be a caregiver, not a controller."

The following journal entries elaborate how an understanding teacher can make a difference in a student's attitude toward education:

a. Suggestions are nothing more than practical ideas about how to initiate a positive trend in academic success, as researcher also acknowledged.

b. Santamaria stated that Mexican students in one study stayed in school because of strong ties to caring and understanding teachers and suggested that due to the high dropout rates in Mexican secondary schools, affectivity must not be overlooked as a means to retain students.

c. The data taught me that in the Mexican culture, when a person is dressed poorly it means that poorly dressed person does not re- spect the other people with whom they are interacting.

This data helped me to understand why my attention to my overall dress and physical appearance inside my public school classroom had such a strong effect on my Mexican students and their parents.

Evaluation

The results of my research will stimulate your thinking. You have in your hands the tools you need to change history by changing lives. Information within these pages will make your time teaching Latinos more satisfying and productive.

Careful about what you assume (evaluate) to be true.

Public schooling is available for all ages and all abilities in Latin America, but the data shows that it was not free and often physically or financially inaccessible. Parents are held responsible for covering the costs of daily transportation, meals, uniforms, and school supplies. These are costs that subsistence farmers are not able to meet, so children often stay home to work instead.

- Don't assume a child who has attended school in Latin America is at US Standards for grade level.
- Don't assume that is a child is not doing well the parents don't care about the child's education.
- Remain a student of life, not judge and jury. Learn about your student's culture.

Challenges

This workbook was written because all children deserve access to a quality education, and all educators deserve to have both the authority and the responsibility to give them that education.

Teachers are failing to teach immigrant students of rural Latino heritage not because the teachers are incompetent, but because the administrative directives for teaching second-language learners are not research-based or appropriate for Native Latinos.

In rural Latin America, teachers usually come to the rural community solely to teach; then they catch a bus home. The teachers lack a social class connection to the community. Their commitment to the community often appears as little more than a means to gain a paycheck.

The complexity of the questions related to what can be done to change those statistics continue to haunt us as we continue to utilize the deficit model of looking at what is wrong with the students, instead of looking in the mirror to see what educators are doing to the students to defeat them.

Planning

Educators have the responsibility for ensuring their students' retention of learned material, but often lack the authority to use evidence-based or scientifically researched teaching methods in their own classrooms.

Professional development classes frequently profess to be helping teachers to obtain better student assessment results. The material the instructors are told to follow, however, is often flawed, inaccurate, misleading, and biased. It works against the teachers' best academic efforts.

I have taken the position that the time has come to step back from rapid-fire, drastic, non-research-based changes, laws, and rules. Instead, we should adopt a proactive view and explain some of the complex questions facing modern education administrators across Latin America and the U.S.

Data revealed that the women appeared to crave knowledge.

I assure you that not expecting your Spanish-speaking students to reach their highest potential is a disservice to them and to their community, as well as to your employer and to your country.

Educators or instructors must rise above the general population with every student and expect the student's best performance under culturally appropriate guidance.

Communists spread the same propaganda about the Polish3 as is currently being spread about Mexicans: lazy, stupid, funny-talking.

The question, "Why on earth would anyone dress down?" must be on the mind of Mexicans when they hear or see this practice in the U.S.

PART TWO

Guided Learning

2

Exerts: The Role of Mothers

"It's always been a pleasure to be around you and pick up these truths that fall from you like ripened fruit from a tree."

—DANA VICTORSTON

The following information is from the textbook titled "Empowering Spanish Speakers—Answers for Educators, Business People, and Friends of Latinos" Chapter 7—The Role of Mothers. Please realize that these are "truths that have fallen from their lips like ripened fruit from a tree," I, as a social scientist, simply gathered them up and now offer them back to you. If you, as an educator, absorb this information, you will benefit every Latino child you teach.

Social Expectations of Latina Mothers

Research found that the resourcefulness of the indigenous mother is nothing short of awe-inspiring. Her creative skills are fine-tuned by basic survival efforts. Living in the campo every day is a test of physical, mental, and emotional endurance, the level of which is not imaginable to mothers in non-third-world countries. A mother in a developed country worries about getting the latest electronic gadget (a new laptop) for her teenage son, paying car insurance premiums for her college-attending daughter, or helping her son prepare for his middle-school Latin final. A campo mother has daily worries about

13

whether there will be enough clean water or cornmeal to make torti-llas to fill the bellies of her six hungry children, whether she will be able to pay the equivalent of $4 a month for her electric bill to keep the single light bulb in her house working, and whether her daugh-ter's only school blouse will be torn by the barbed-wire clothesline during a windstorm. All mothers have concerns for their children's welfare. However, campo mothers are fighting for their children's ba-sic physical survival, while mothers in developed countries are

negotiating for their children's social standing. The social status concerns of a mother in a developed country are perceived by her as being strongly connected to access to educational opportunities and elevated social status.

Caregiver is the Rural Latina Mother's Central Role

The social expectation for the rural mother is to be the caregiver, primarily of children. She is expected to be wholly committed to her role, with or without a partner. Mothers appear to have clearly de-fined roles as caregivers of their children; very few work outside the house, drive a car, or are involved in any activity other than staying in the house or walking to the house of another relative to care for him or her.

The following is an excerpt from Maria's interview:

QUESTION: So, could I say that you feel like you've really succeeded in your life, that you feel really good about your life?

MARIA: I have succeeded, but I have not accomplished yet what I want for them (the children)—but I think I have succeeded.

QUESTION: It is (through) them (i.e. how they, the children, are doing in life)—that's how you rate yourself. It's (through) them, is that right?

MARIA: That is how I rate myself. I knew that since they were small, a reflection of me was going to be in them. I know that each one of them has to be them (an indi- vidual), and that is the way I want it.

Single Head of Household

All too often the indigenous mother's absent husband forgets to send money; he might stay away for years, while she waits. It is her fate as the caregiver to simply wait—that is the role the females born in the campo assume. Mothers, with or without husbands working lo- cally, stay home and work from early in the morning until late in the evening every day to care for the family. The level of care taken to clean the houses is excessive by U.S. norms, perhaps because the wa- ter is not potable and always cold. Mothers spend seemingly endless hours scrubbing both the insides and the outsides of their houses with powerful disinfectants. Most houses are cleaned with a single strong product; the smell of "Fabuloso" permeates the air each morning in the urban cities.

The Women's Struggle for Healthy Families

Despite great care and caution being taken to keep intestinal para- sites out of the food, children often get very sick. Other researchers found that the Latina mothers interviewed "promoted and protected the health of their preschool children by taking care ('el cuidado') and by being mindful ('el pendiente') of balancing the health of their infants', children's,' and youths' bodies, minds, and souls." I discov- ered that by understanding this personal cultural outlook, it might be possible to design culturally sensitive health programs that would reach toward and build on existing maternal strengths. If urban and rural women were reached in a heritage-appropriate manner and if the offered programs acknowledged their children as the national treasures, the living assets, and the future leaders of Latin America, then the women might be able to understand the value of exerting a greater effort toward preventative health care. They could, for ex- ample, learn how to reduce the use of sugar, restrict processed foods, and increase home vegetable gardening. My observations and sug- gestions are consistent with those of other researchers.

Summary: The Role of Latina Women

It is hard to remain unbiased when observing Latina girls, women, grandmothers, and the role into which they are born. Their culture demands youthful domestic responsibilities at a very early age and unimaginable responsibilities of motherhood, but does not allow equality with the males. At a very early age, frequently by 4 years of age, girls are wobbling on rather high heels and wearing red lipstick with tight jeans and dangling earrings, because that is the norm within the culture. As mothers, they often look totally worn out due to bearing many children. By old age, they have lost height due to physically carrying anywhere from eight to over a dozen children both inside and outside their wombs, as well as emotionally carrying much domestic responsibility. They are, indeed, to be both admired and assisted, but only when they specifically request help. They are proud women and deserve the utmost respect and the most culturally appropriate emotional, educational, and physical support.

Conclusion:

To understand preschool through middle school Latino children is to know the highest level of education attained by 90% of today's Latino adults living in rural areas. When a Latino rural-raised child finishes grade six, seven, or eight, he or she will act like they are done with any formal education that they will need for their entire life. It matter little what the law says about how much schooling a child must receive; this is a sociocultural fact. It is your responsibility, as an educator, to change that deeply rooted cultural attitude.

3 Executive Functions

English speakers say, "I missed the bus." Spanish speakers say, "The bus left me!" It is evident everywhere that Latinos lack executive functions.

—Dr. Helena Todd

Diverse

The following instructions throughout this guide will not make sense without some background as to why I am making the suggestions I am for obtaining success when teaching Latino children.

Why do Asians find academic success in U.S. schools and Latinos don't?

The simple answer is that Asians typically learn in classrooms in Japan, China, and Taiwan. Long hours are spent being instructed and doing writing and reading. There are long periods of indoor work broken up by extensive recess outdoors where learning is not occurring. Researcher Harold W. Stevenson is quoted as saying, "The recess in turn fosters a positive attitude towards academics," *which takes place indoors with verbal interactions - just like in the US.*

The Asian approach to education is more complex:

1. Asian **families** believe that a child's primary role is their schoolwork. An Asian child's existence is focused on their education. The parents are extremely involved in reinforcing that role as exclusive and primary to their children to gain independence, a career, and an adult life of their choosing.

2. The Asian states set the **educational standards** clearly and quantifiable, perhaps to a fault. No person is left without a total understanding of what is acceptable; there are no exceptions. In the US the teacher is the authoritarian figure with which there is conflict about what work is to be done. In Asia, the teacher is a coach who is doing his or her best to help each student meet the unrelenting standards known by the students, teachers, parents, and every community member.

3. **The school day** is about 8 hours a day plus homework. There are long breaks to walk home to eat, have extra activities, individual reading periods, and recess outdoors for socialization. The school is the focus of the student's life. Children want more education for themselves, not more assets for public viewing and admiration.

4. **Teachers are coaches** of Asian children. The students are often engaged in their own learning using "manipulatives" (especially in math class) and work centers focusing on one area of interest. The act of learning becomes main entertainment for children of all ages.

5. **Teaching methods** are not boring. The student's entire focus is on gaining knowledge. Parents and teachers reinforce that concept. Students are encouraged at home and in school to process concepts in a verbal manner with their parents and other siblings.

The rural Latino (those who are most likely to immigrate to the US to seek a quality education) approach to education is extremely different:

1. Latino rural **families** believe that a child's primary role is to economically assist in the basic survival of the family. Children as young as two years old will help to support the family's income needs. A rural Latino child's existence is focused on the most primary needs of the family: food, shelter, clothing, and healthcare. The parents are extremely involved in reinforcing the role of interdependent provider and protector of the immediate family as exclusive and primary of their children for the offspring's entire lifetime. Every child is expected to marry, have children, and expand the family in an interdependent manner.

2. The Mexican federal government sets the **educational standards** with a wide range of interpretation. No person knows when rural schools are closed for teacher's meetings, what time teachers arrive, there are no substitute teachers, there is a significant shortage of supplies, there is no food break, the school day is very short, there are no teacher's aids or volunteer parents in the schools, the coursework does not relate to rural life, few assets for special needs students, and parents are rarely in the classroom or involved in the academic activities in any way. Parents do not consider it their job to teach anything that is taught in the school system. In school, business, or politics, there are always exceptions in Latin America based on status, networking, or the payment of bribes. In the US the teacher is the authoritarian figure with which there is conflict about what work is to be done. In Latin America, the teacher is from a higher social status and just their presence intimidates adults and children. The teacher is doing his or her best to help each student stay occupied by rote memory writing. Teachers often complain that the tests do not reflect what the curricula dictates what be taught to the students. The students, teachers, parents, and/or no community members know what criteria are used to evaluate a student related to reaching academic standards. Gaining a higher education does **not** elevate social status until three generations have

achieved the same or higher degrees. Therefore, there is little reason to pursue education as a means to improve their lives.

3. **The school day** is about 5 hours a day—8 A.M. to 1 P.M. Students do not have homework because they have a variety of domestic and/or farm chores at home. During the 5 hours school day, one hour is allocated for eating food brought to school or sold by visiting mothers on the school grounds. The there is recess outdoors for socialization. The student's home and church is the focus of the student's life. The boys are poor students because they are not learning how to make more money for the family. Principals and teachers alike tell us that boy students' only dream of running north to the USA border to make their fortune. The girls are outstanding students until about the age of 12 or 13 when they realize that time is running out to get a local boy to marry them. Most of the rural communities lack males; the boys and men are working elsewhere. Students feel hopeless and caught in the rural dead end. They want more status symbols for public viewing—MP3 players, cell phones, rhinestones anywhere possible, fancy shoes and/or other clothing—to feel higher self-esteem. Subsistence farmer's children are on the last—the 14th—level of social status. Assets are used to overcome the feelings of hopelessness..

4. **Teachers are unconsciously intimidating** of Latino children and their families. Teachers had family money usually borrowed from family members make it possible for them to attend college. Teachers come from a higher social status than their rural students.

5. **Teaching methods** are boring. The students copy pages of text, much of which they do not understand, for endless hours. The act of learning becomes a horrid boring part of the day until grade 5 or 6 for children of all ages. The student's entire focus is watching the clock free them to go home. Parents reinforce that concept because any child in school is a pair of hands not helping make some income for the family. Students learn by mimicking their elders and sibling—verbal exchange is limited with both their parents and other siblings.

Undeveloped

Anytime a person can get in and out of a bank in less than one hour, something very unusual must have occurred.

The greatest resource in Latin America is the ability to survive today in joyful celebration of life in spite of promises of gloom on tomorrow's horizon.

Culturally unaware observers cannot help but be mystified at the re-sil- ience of Latinos exhibiting such unusual carefree behavior when so much in these Latinos' lives is not free of many cares.

As I observed life in the campo, it seemed as though while economic or political news told of cities figuratively burning to the ground, in rural Latin America music played, relationships were nurtured, bright colors further enhanced the richness of the landscape, and good food was relished among friends and families.

The simple fact remained that there was nothing socially powerless people could do or wanted to do to save the cities and their unpredictable politics.

Unscheduled closing of the entire school or individual classrooms often occurred. Without any funding or administrative policy allocating money for substitute teachers, there was often a lack of supervision and even a lack of teaching in classes I visited if a teacher was absent.

Educators or instructors need to understand that little regard is given to maintaining published school schedules in rural Latin America. This is also true of backup plans for substitute teachers that are needed to maintain the flow of learning when a teacher is absent. With that as the norm, how can a dedicated teacher in the U.S. or in Latin America expect Latinos to comprehend the value of education? It is your job to educate the student not only with content (school curricula or corpo-rate training), but also with appropriate procedures necessary to gain a quality education or a promotion. The student probably has never had a mentor to explain what it takes to be academically successful.

Self-discipline is certainly a valuable trait for students to acquire.

The child was learning self-discipline, patience, and teamwork in both places. However, the subjects taught at school were about life outside of the community, while the lessons presented at home were related to home life, family business, extended family needs, and community affairs.

The total cost for Salsite's school uniform was $120 (USD), which is equivalent to 240 hours of work for a parent in a minimum-wage job. Minimum wage in Mexico was 50 pesos a day, or about $0.50 an hour.

The willingness to lose money in order to accommodate the employees' need for a relationship was, for this researcher, a major social statement. (This tip is in this workbook twice—understanding the investment in a relationship with people is paramount to understanding this culture)

Compared to U.S. residents, Latinos are very far-sighted with regard to accepting fate or karma. Latinos will refuse to sell family land, believing that their fate is to protect this land. They will accept a loss of life, believing that the person's karma led him or her to die young. They do not exercise executive functions, such as planning ahead, well. It is hard for a Latino of faith to study for several years and spend lots of tuition money without first knowing his fate.

If a potential Latino student felt a sign from God, he might make an academic commitment—but God has already assured him that family comes first. He knows that it takes an average of three generations of educated people to raise social status. Most Latinos would not put their family aside and their career or education first for that length of time.

There were little or no printed materials in the rural Latinos' homes. After the age of about 12, most teens or adults had no access to books.

4 Responsibility & Discipline

The difficulties experienced by immigrant students indicate that cross-cultural differences in cognition are most probably related to learning practices characteristic of different culture(s)....These differences can be observed not only between cultures but also within a given culture.

—ALEX KOZULEN (1998)

Denial—Intimidated

The book *Subtractive Schooling*, written by Angelica Valenzuela, gives an excellent example of the harm that can be done to students as a result of classroom or curriculum mismanagement. Instead of adding to their knowledge base in the classroom, students slip behind when the language of the instruction is not understood. The same situation can occur when a person is *improperly labeled*.

The Latin American government provides some supplemental nutritional aid. There exists a lack of adequate nutrients. Malnutrition is so common that both children and adults require nutritional supplements. In my research, I found that 30.9% of the 665 examined children suffered negative side effects from malnutrition; these findings are very similar to what others have found.

According to Child Welfare Information Gateway, the brain of a child is 90% developed to adult size by the age of three. There is a strong likelihood that many of the pre-school through middle school age Latino children you are teaching were malnourished as infants. Teach nutrition (1) in classroom lessons, (2) by example with what you eat in front of them or give to them to eat, (3) make sure they receive any free meals offered at your school, (4) and do all you can to make sure their mothers have access to information on nutrition.

The indigenous caregiver simply cannot complete the paperwork adequately, nor is he or she able to pay additional fees, in the form of a mordita, for approval with errors; a bribe is often necessary to overlook an error or omission. Another contributing factor is the applicant's the inability to fill out a form due to illiteracy; research data estimated rural illiteracy to be at 50%.6 Lack of reading skills usually reduces economic stability, making the need for assistance greater.

The rural medical personnel I interviewed verified that in spite of mothers' best efforts, malnutrition is a regional epidemic. Additionally, most children have acid reflux and intestinal parasites.

"Hopeless" was the adjective that best described what I heard from adults.

Children are given a long string of names, usually five or six of distinctive value. That unique combination makes them very unique and identifies them specifically.

Several people I interviewed told me that 12 was the standard age of consent for a girl. Therefore, unless a girl is younger than 12 years of age, she is presumed to have agreed to have sex.

Few women in this culture are willing to accept the role of speaking out for and protecting women's rights.

Access to transportation is a major factor in determining the economic positioning of an entire community.

Confusion—Self-Doubt

In school, students were expected to copy endless pages of printed material by hand while sitting at desks, tables, or in other group settings where they could talk among themselves, comfortably walk around the room, help each other with lessons, solve problems together, and freely exchange ideas. This often took place in a multi-leveled classroom. The classrooms were always crowded. The desks or tables were touching, personal space was very tight, and there were up to 55 students with one teacher.

Data suggested that Native Indian or indigenous Laatino caregivers struggle with self-esteem issues related to social class status and, thus, fail to advocate for themselves or their children in the U.S., as well as in Latin America.

Life in rural Latin America has ritual woven into most aspects of living. People use faith to overcome adversity and tragedy.

The high class Latina and the Native Latina mothers are worlds apart (14 social levels), and so are their children. Understanding this difference is a major factor in comprehending why academic success for Latino children is frequently a significant challenge.

I observed that speech in rural Latin America is generally saved for other adults. Teamwork in outlying Latin America is coordinated visually more than verbally. Even among adults, fewer words are used than is common for verbalizing in other cultures in their home countries.

Malnutrition and sociocultural disadvantages have been found to increase the clinical characteristics of learning disabilities or other special needs in socioeconomically disadvantaged Latino children.

Frustration – Depression

At home in Latin America, children were expected to ask questions of each other, practice learned behavior, function within a "non-stressful domain or neutral zone of comfort, where little criticism was expressed, and they were not faulted,...allowing self-evaluation and self-judgment"; they were also encouraged to take as long as they liked to accomplish the task.22 This is in sharp contrast to the continuous deadline constraints placed on children in the U.S. public schools.

The woman gets the family ahead (i.e. she becomes the family leader, head of household, [and] takes charge) after the woman gets pregnant and the man leaves.

The Latino male can leave his family, leave his job, not attend church, and behave in a manner inside his community that is less than honorable, and yet his social status is relatively unharmed. It is not their responsibility to think about it [their behavior], do anything about their behavior, or take any credit or blame for how it turns out.

The parents reported that children were expected to speak softly and infrequently; any other behavioral pattern was an alert of grave concern. I expected children to be talkative and active with adults or other children. How I expected a child to communicate and act in the presence of an adult and how I expected a child to behave when playing with another child were far outside of the parameters expected by rural mothers.

If a child does not talk and a specialist perceives that to be a verbal disability, this may be an invalid assessment. Instead, cultural influences or other factors may be present.

Anger—Defensive

In the U.S., students are nearly always working alone, in competition with other students, while sitting at an individual desk—not in a group setting that is common in Latin America. Additionally, in the U.S., the students are not allowed to talk with each other in class; they are not allowed to walk over to another student's desk to get clarification, information, or to exchange ideas. In fact, if the student asked another student a question, the one who spoke up and was heard by the teacher would likely be severely punished, and may even be accused of cheating!

Having no social security or retirement provisions appeared to cause the women to expect absolute obedience from their children, in order to instill the belief that caring for elderly parents was absolutely paramount.

It is not appropriate for life-skills educators or trainers to assume that rural Latina women know how to clean a home or a business in urban areas or per the U.S. standards. If the school is teaching life skills or a job is to include cleaning, then training of how to clean a modern home or an office should be provided.

Worldwide, 3- to 5-year-old indigenous children largely care for themselves23 and often at least one younger sibling. If a child has had all of that responsibility from the age of 3 or 5, is it any wonder that being treated like a helpless and irresponsible young child as a teenager generates anger and resentment?

Researchers Norma González, Luis Moll, and Cathy Amanti found that the use of the schooling model of punitive measures and time limits within learning situations "developed one of the few adult-child conflicts within the household." These same three researchers suggested that reduced self-esteem was the outcome of the punitive measures model of schooling, because of the cultural conflict of expectations that opposed the student-motivated style of learning of the Latino culture. Educators or instructors would do well to rework the student syllabi to be more student-friendly or to develop student-driven learning syllabi.

Children were expected to ask questions and practice the learned behavior, functioning within a "non-stressful domain or neutral zone of comfort, where little criticism was expressed, and they would not be faulted. "As a result, "this more relaxed approach allowed self-evaluation and self-judgment." The students were also encouraged to take as long as they liked to accomplish the task, which was a better approach for Latino students.

Quitting—Detachment

If a family manages to have three generations of people both gain a professional education and gain financial success, only then does the social status of the family improve. Those I interviewed agreed that the higher-class social acceptance must be based on common elements of economic stability, education, and career title, and that at least two of these must be present for at least three generations.

The social status of a family improves only if the family manages to have three generations of people both gain a professional education and gain financial success. Those I interviewed agreed that the higher-class social acceptance must be based on common elements of financial success, education, and career title, and that at least two of these must be present for at least three generations.

Domestic violence and incest are often overlooked by both sexes and the public as a "normal" aspect of life in Latin America.

Educators or instructors of Spanish speakers should consider that a lack of supportive commitment to students might be a deterrent to creating a positive learning environment.

Latina mothers appear to have an innate knowledge of how to make a child feel loved. Latina mothers want their children to have high self-esteem, to have self-love, to develop a deeply rooted sense of responsibility to succeed in school, and to become capable, humble, accepting, and productive adults.

The word that was lacking in that description was happy. I observed that Latinos work to find joy, because they live in a fatalistic society. Unlike the American dream, where anything is possible, the attitude overwhelmingly apparent in rural Latin America is: Today was hard and tomorrow may never come.

We (U.S.) have the most prolonged adolescence in the history of mankind. There is no other society that requires so many years to pass before people are grown up. Adolescence is nurtured and prolonged by educational processes and by industry that has found a bonanza embracing the teenaged population and fortifying "adolescent values." This prolongation of adolescence robs the country of the population group (currently the Millennial Generation) having the most risk takers, and the highest ideals.

Several mothers asked for suggested ways out of the demands required by their campesino lifestyle.

5 Motivation & Encouragement

Don't handicap your children by making their lives easy.

—Robert A. Heinlein

Challenges

Consider the following advice: Treat all children with Response to Intervention (RTI) I techniques or with the same consideration that the U.S. law provides to the disabled student. All students will benefit.

Parents had no energy left in their lives to concern themselves with what children might have wanted outside of adequate food, dry shelter, and warm clothing for the winter.

The disadvantages included depravation of overall basic needs, alcoholism, depression, incest, domestic violence, poor health, inadequate nutrition, and increased illness risk.

Independence, Development, and Crawling

Infants are held day and night until they walk, which means they are not allowed to crawl. I observed this phenomenon in cities, in vil- lages, in health clinics, and in homes from all socioeconomic levels. I questioned parents, medical personnel, and teachers to make certain I was correct; all agreed crawling is not culturally sanctioned. A female physician, the mother of six who was educated in the U.S., allowed me to interview her about crawling. She assured me that keeping Latino children off dirt or bare concrete floors is probably only one reason for not allowing children to crawl. She explained that cultural tradition requires that an older person physically controls an infant at all times. She confirmed my observations that infants are rarely out of a parents', siblings', or another relatives' arms night or day; infants are normally wrapped tightly in layered blankets that allow restricted movement. She explained that only one of her children had crawled. She elaborated by saying that quizzical stares toward both her and her infant confirmed that people found both the child's behavior and her allowing that behavior to occur very odd. Additionally, she added that in her lifetime, she had never seen another Latino infant crawl; she was nearly 40 years of age at the time.

Researchers vary from having very strong proactive opinions to site concerns about infants not receiving benefits from crawling. Research results are mixed related to developmental movement therapy programs that incorporate crawling or crawling-like behavior by children or adults (long after learning to walk). Most experts agree that crawling increases muscle strength, balance, and eye-hand coordination. Additionally, crawling stimulates brain activity, the ability to perceive and comprehend the depth (an understanding of edges, ledges, and falling), left and right brain coordination, and increased oxygen flow throughout the body, specifically to the brain. Emotionally, it increases independence by stimulating the crawler's willingness to independently explore the surrounding environment.

Crawling certainly increases independence and personal decision-making. Latino infants are nearly always held. Traditionally, they do not independently crawl and explore on their own. Therefore, their level of independence is reduced compared to the U.S. standards, and they have almost no decision-making opportunities. Educators or instructors should consider that this might have some positive influence with regard to family bonding and some negative influence with regard to independence.

Latin America has a totally different history. After Spain conquered Mexico and took control from Native Indians, other countries were expected to steal the "New Spain," Mexico. The governments of Spain and other neighboring countries were, for hundreds of years, under the rule of a very complex hierarchy of monarchs. These monarchs were absolute rulers, conquers, and warriors.

The public message was that people who overpowered others and took their property increased their own and their country's wealth. The appearance of how business was done and the means to financial success were to pillage from others with total disregard for others' property.

Due to life being so uncertain, only what was needed for today was purchased for today. Rarely was there planning ahead for the following day's meal or for the next step in a construction project.

In the same manner that we traveled great distances by car to reach rural campos, most teachers traveled great distances by bus from their urban homes to reach a school in the campos.

We were informed that this could result in lack of consistent attendance by teachers, and that there were no substitute teachers available to take over the duties.

Children functioned alone in the classroom when the teacher was absent. The urban teacher was a person of status; the rural child was a campesino. We observed first hand that the children did not command much respect from their teachers.

Within the primary grades, having 40 or more students with one teacher in one classroom was common; having 80 or 90 students with one teacher occurred too frequently.

Life-long malnutrition adds to the difficulties faced when an indigenous rural Latino child attends school to gain an education; fortunately, this can be overcome with an adequate diet.

Identities

Students love being appreciated, receiving respect, doing activities that build on what they know, and working as equals with other peers.

The word "sociocultural", according to Lev Vygotsky, is "the genetic law of cultural development—any function of a child's cultural development that appears on a social plane while simultaneously appearing on a psychological plane is sociocultural."

This narrow domestic assignment is not a shared responsibility with the husband or a son—only with a daughter, sister, or another female.

"I am much harder on my girls! I have to be, because our culture expects so much more of them. They have so much more responsibility than the men. All the man has to do is earn money."

The woman must do whatever it takes to care for the family, to keep the children safe, to make the home—whatever it takes. That is why all Latina women must be strong.

"They (Latinos) love the boys more. It is the girls who raise the babies and run the households." (direct quote)

The Latino male can leave his family, leave his job, not attend church, and behave in a manner inside his community that is less than honorable, and yet his social status is relatively unharmed.

"A man is 'Dad' in name only; the mother is the actual head of every Latino household." (direct quote)

Boys would never be asked to help with anything that the women were doing, but it was common to see the women help the boys with cleaning.

Employees were expected to watch each other to make sure that nothing was stolen and that no one ever made a mistake. The primary business focus seemed to be on employees monitoring each other, not on customer service. The effect on clients was painful, because time spent waiting was excessive by the U.S. standards.

Additional people checked the work completed by the first employee at least twice before moving on. There was no margin of error planned into business practices in Latin America.

Rewards

Statistics have shown that nearly half of all Latino immigrant children living in the U.S. and attending public schools did not graduate from high school, although they were expected to complete the program. Other studies have shown that many Latinos were motivated to finish since they had set life goals that relied on graduating from high school.

The women within the scope of my research lived outdoors for a large percentage of each day—cooking, eating, bathing, washing clothing, caring for domestic livestock, walking to school or neighborhood vendors, socializing in multi-generational settings, worshiping, and interacting informally with peers. Women are always caring for others, but they are not learning any new ways to accomplish this task.

You cannot get a check cashed in Latin America— there is always a reason found to turn down cashing a check. One expatriate actually wrote someone a check at the bank in front of a teller immediately after signing the bank's signature card, but the check was still refused because the signatures were not totally identical. No kidding. The person immediately closed the bank account.

There will be a minimum of three trips required to the immigration office to get the paperwork completed, unless a university or a corporation applies for you in your name. It can take a year, but if the university or the corporation has the right connections or pays a bribe ("mordita"), then the visa will be issued.

Experiments

A culturally appropriate approach leads the student toward positive results, such as high self-esteem, engagement, active learning, academic success, and graduation from high school.

It is the high regard for children in general and the cultural view in particular that cause all adults within the extended family to care for the children.

In 40 months of living in the campo, I observed only one person over 50 reading a book at home. He was the town mayor and was reading the Bible.

There was no after-school tutoring, as students were needed at home to help with the farming or other chores.

Incorporation

This workbook was written to enable you, the reader, to easily extract information and guidelines to follow. I call these guidelines techniques of positive change; they can help you empower students of Latino heritage, by acknowledging and enhancing their life experiences, in order to enrich their continued academic success.

I undertook this research and lifestyle with a high level of commitment because I was seeking to understand Latino sociocultural influences on human development. Admittedly, the factors I think I understand will continue to change. Researcher Barbara Rogoff explains that sociocultural influences on human development "can be understood only in light of the cultural practices and circumstance of their communities—which also change." Similar to a housewife's circumstance, this type of research can never be finished, as it continuously evolves.

The extended family provides cooperation and mutual support. What works satisfactorily within the family unit will work equally well in schools if lessons in each subject are a cooperative effort.5 Do not assume this extends into the community. The defined family unit is inwardly focused.

Teachers in Latin America are always touching Latino children; this probably helps the children to overcome some emotional challenges that exist. Immigrant Latino students must be confused and disoriented in U.S. schools, where touch is prohibited in educational environments.

It is typical of the Latino culture for children to handle adult-sized responsibilities at home. When language use forces the student into yet another adult role, keep in mind that if you as educators or instructors expect less of them at school or in the workplace, you lessen that adult level of respect toward them and their capabilities. Such an action reduces self-esteem. Don't be guilty of this social offence!

Families

Historically, Latinos have fought long and hard in the U.S. and in Latin America for educational reform for their children. They were very active in the Chicano Rights Movement of the 1960s and 1970s, but had less publicity than the Black Power Movement (1966–1975).1

A great deal of rural family pride went into sending a child to school. The emphasis was on appearance and behavior.

Latino parents did not consider themselves to be responsible at any level for the child's school performance or to be the primary teachers of the child.

The line between teachers and parents was clearly defined by years of tradition. Rarely did parents ever help teachers in any way.

After all that I have observed, I cannot imagine why U.S. citizens continue to say that Latino parents don't value education. Clearly massive amounts of time, energy, money, and family efforts are involved in making it possible for a child to attend school, especially middle school and higher, in Latin America. The confusion, I think, arises due to the difference between the Latino standards and the U.S. standards in defining the expected parent and teacher roles. The following interview with Maria demonstrates how she has adapted to the U.S. Her thought process expresses the "whatever it takes" mind-set common in the U.S., while her focus, due to her Latina heritage, remains on a "good upbringing" for the children, which may or may not include a quality education.

And I would do whatever it takes! To do...to give them that good upbringing. Even if I had to get three jobs, I would do it!

An odd adaptation occurs for Latinos who either move to the U.S. or have relatives who have made that transition. There really is a sense among Latinos that anything is possible and not nearly as difficult to obtain in the U.S., including a quality education. Perhaps this outlook is due to wishful thinking, but it creates an obvious conflict. Any student of ethnography would be amazed and humbled by the optimism of Latino parents that their children would graduate from college if they lived in the U.S. Either the statistical evidence of how few Latinos complete high school or graduate from college is being ignored or the facts are simply not known. Additionally, Latino parents appear to accept the cultural bias problems being faced today and assume that their children will overcome those hurdles.

Many adult immigrants speak exclusively Spanish at home; in school, however, their children's use of language other than English is restricted. A bilingual lifestyle can be confusing for a child. At school, English is mandated; English is the language used for teaching. Some schools even monitor playground communication, restricting the use of languages other than English during recreational breaks.

Children as young as nine years of age are often speaking for anyone in the family who is not fluent in English and making life-changing and legally binding decisions.

Researchers have studied the meal-time conversations of middle-class Caucasian families outside of Latin America and found that their table conversation had a very exacting school-style way of speaking, which allowed children to practice public speaking.

6 Activities & Instruction

Education seems to be in America the only commodity of which the customer tries to get as little he can for his money.

—Max Leon Forman (1909–1990), *Jewish-American writer.*

Creativity

The educators' authorized curricula fails to use a method that builds on the students' background (scaffolding), enhances their self-esteem, and empowers them. This is especially true for those students raised in rural environments. Acknowledging and enhancing their life experiences could enhance learning. Enhanced learning may create happiness in the schools, and happy students are often more motivated to learn.

The data implies that generations of offspring are expected to remain respectful their entire lives, always staying in or near the community to care for their aging parents or grandparents.

All interviewees stated that they lost status within their family by moving and focusing on a world outside their campo.

One Mexican school director stated: "Mexican people are the most creative in the world. They have no social service programs so they must figure out how to earn an income."

Senses

Research has confirmed that children and parents spent little time together in verbal exchanges. One-on-one discussions or detailed descriptions by adults are rarely directed toward children.

Latino students have some major emotional development advantages, because as children they have adult responsibilities that increase maturity. They spend a large portion of each day outdoors, which increases their attention span. They spend little time in front of a TV and even less on the Internet, which decreases their need to be distracted by outside stimulation.

In January 2004, I wrote a thesis titled Outdoor Education for the Development of Responsible Youth at the University of Arizona. This exercise was frustrating because there was a shortage of research material available. Fortunately, a copious amount of academic material related to outdoor education exists today, as many researchers now agree on the value of time in nature for mental, emotional, physical, and spiritual health.

This fact alone serves to reinforce my theory of untapped human resources available in agricultural communities in Latin America. Rural residents appear to have all the right ingredients for success in life; they are simply starving for access to knowledge of life outside the campo and for opportunities anywhere.

Engagement

Researchers have applied methods of training people in workshops with the expectation that performance within the workplace will mirror the workshop experience. They have found that cultural factors interfere with that transfer process. Relating to the existing funds of knowledge helps overcome that problem.

Contact with nature may equal in importance to adequate sleep and good nutrition in order to achieve *mental*, *physical*, and *spiritual health*. *The health of the earth is at stake as well*. It may be that the development of mental, physical, and spiritual health is magnified by the rural *campesino* lifestyle. Those facts might explain the ability of your students to win the struggle for survival and care for their families and extended families, even with an otherwise overwhelming sense of hopelessness.

This business environment is not efficient for the economic growth of a country as a whole: Too much focus is placed on watching the competition at the retail level and not enough on external customer service, internal quality control, design and development of new products, efficiency of operations, marketing, and other executive functions of a successful business model.

Logic dictates that a government that cannot collect taxes cannot supply adequate services to the public.

Nutritional problems were very widespread in rural areas of Central and Western Mexico. Medical personnel confirmed that situation, and several referred to this endemic situation as an epidemic. Poor nutrition influenced school performance.

At home in the campo, parents did not typically verbally correct the children to speak more clearly, nor did they correct subtle body language messages. In contrast to other cultures, rarely did an evening in the campo home include parents giving their children verbal lessons.

What each teacher or trainer must understand is that the way any faith is practiced must be taken into consideration in order to best enable teaching techniques to be effective and compatible with the students' religious beliefs.

Data implies that *campesino* children are educationally marginalized because of their cultural status; other researchers have obtained the same results. *There is ample evidence that children from these social class backgrounds are limited by their schooling, by the nature of the instruction that they receive.*

Teamwork

In the outdoors, the students are using adult tools and are not overly protected or supervised. They are making and correcting their own mistakes, and learning from them. They are not following detailed spoken instructions typical of a sterile classroom.

Teamwork in outdoor environments is seen throughout the workday.

Qualitative data told the same story—that as each woman started her shift at the school, she took the time to greet every other woman with a hug and a kiss on the cheek, and then to inquire about their respective families. The culture dictated this form of physical and emotional contact.

The women I interviewed in the Arizona school shouldered a collective understanding of how deadly the road they walked along and lived on really was. This road commonly referred to as the open wound, was on the border between the U.S. and Latin America.

The women in the campo, work as a team; most are related, or have been related at one time or another. Collectively, the women find a way to keep a level head because of their strong faith in God and each other. Their hearts are always ready to accept yet another child who needs them.

Much of the rural Latinos' lives are intertwined with both internal and external cultural, social, political, and religious events, because there is a "trickle-down" effect within this economically and socially depressed society. Economic and/or social changes in the upper classes have a direct effect on the lower classes. What they do not lack is creativity and innovation.

What I did not understand then was that within the hierarchic political structure of the Latino government, in which a new president is elected every six years, is a system of overwhelming change based almost exclusively on the relationship factor.

Students were normally given copies of the tests that they would take later and given the answers to multiple-choice or other test questions ahead of the assessment. They then copied the information until they learned the answer to the specific question—the exact question they would see on the test. They also copied pages of text, seemingly endlessly, to absorb the correct information. The students always helped each other.

Assessment

As a result, a Latino adult's or child's level of interest, ambition, or involvement in matters of business or social life outside of the immediate home is often negligible; it frequently does not even extend into their local community.

In nature and in a primitive camping style of daily living, children develop an increased demand for cognitive thinking skills.[8] This development appears to be due to the need to react quickly in order to survive potentially life-threatening situations.

Educators or instructors need to understand that time spent outdoors has been reduced a great deal in our time.

> *This new symbolic demarcation line suggests that baby boomers—Americans born between 1946 and 1964—may constitute the last generation of Americans to share an intimate, familial attachment to the land and water.*

All rural and urban public school classrooms I observed in Mexico lacked basic resources, including such simple amenities as adequate bathrooms.

Observers of the rural world learn firsthand just how hard the whole process of obtaining a quality education becomes for the children of subsistence farmers. Actual academic activities in school occurred for about three hours each day—not enough to give the children the quality education they deserve.

Each multigenerational person is likely to have **community literacy** or **cultural literacy** stemming from the funds of knowledge gained by understanding the rituals and acceptable behaviors in of his campo (community) and comprehending its norms.

Of the younger adults under the age of 25, most stated that those in the campo usually only attended primary school until the fifth or sixth grade. Data indicated that the dreams of the children in the campo have more to do with an income for survival and less to do with careers, as the following journal entry points out:

> The majority of young teenage boys of public school age stated that all they wanted was to go to the U.S. for work—work that was manual labor. More young teenage girls applied themselves to reading and classroom studies. The girls exhibited behaviors that made it clear (that) they understood education as a pathway out of life-long poverty and mandatory motherhood.

When asked, caregivers and students replied that they had no access to a library or the Internet for information.

Historically policymakers at the federal administrative or school district levels have shown little regard for evidence-based or scientifically based data. The following direct quote makes that historical position clear:

> High-quality empirical research can guide policy. Admittedly, due to the disconnect between the research base and policymaking, that potential is often squandered. The mere existence of careful, rigorous research makes little impact if policymakers remain oblivious or if lesser-quality work is more effectively communicated and advocated.

PART THREE

Student Outcome

7 Assessments

"No problem can be solved by the same consciousness that created it. We need to see the world anew"

—ALBERT EINSTEIN

The Winners Circle

For their children to have access to an education, it is vital for Latina mothers to gain access to knowledge first and to maintain such access on an ongoing basis. Educated mothers educate their children, even if only by the children's observation of their mothers reading or doing a math calculation. Uneducated mothers are unable to help their children with schoolwork. Even though the culture does not encourage mothers to accept the role of an educator, educated women will influence their children's education in a positive manner.

Qualitative data analysis implied that only a few reoccurring developmental delays (i.e. starting to talk very late and being unable to crawl) were directly related to cultural influences.

Not all Latinos will become famous authors, Web engineers, or programmers, but most will find a way to earn a living that will financially outpace what they can currently earn in Latin America. More importantly, in a culture where the work of an ancestor is honored, their children will have the same opportunities to economically improve their lives in the very next generation.

Until the percentage of Hispanic leaders in positions of political power and financial influence equals the same percentage of Hispanic people living in the U.S., a mismatch exists; it is a wrong that is in dire need of correction.

Lifetime Relationships

Historical, social, and cultural reasons may attribute to Latino students' frequent failure to attain educational gratification and honors in Latin America and the U.S. Feuerstein's Mediated Learning Experience (MLE) theory, the belief in human modifiability based on a socio- cultural influence, was the best explanation I found to address why many students of Latino heritage find academic success to be eva- sive in both countries.

The MLE theory includes regulation and control of behavior, feelings of competency (displaying what one knows), sharing behavior (teaching each other in groups), individuation or psychological differentiation (appreciating the similarities and differences in each other), and self-driven goal of seeking-setting-achieving-monitoring (a learner-based creation of each course syllabus); the students are responsible for creating their own syllabus

Rural Latino children's conscientious behavior may be influenced by mediated learning experiences associated with their native culture. In an agricultural area, most of the learning continues to take place outdoors by observing and mimicking the activities of adults.

Each child at the U.S. school was patiently held, rubbed, or verbally soothed, while soft music played in the background—no one knew what physical, mental, or emotional challenges that tiny soul faced elsewhere. Eventually, all of the children would fall asleep; they always did. Some children who experienced challenging home lives slept for 2 to 3 hours in that place of love and safety, while others slept for just 30 to 40 minutes.

Kingsolver remarked, "What I discovered in Spain was a culture that held children to be its meringues and éclairs." The same is true in rural Central Mexico, where children are **participants in dynamic cultural communities**, where they are constantly held, admired, and highly cherished.

The Latino infant is constantly being touched, shifted, or checked on while hearing another's heartbeat. Additionally, if children start to cry while being held, their needs are met immediately to help them stop crying.

I observed that unlike European-American **packaged** babies, Latino infants often have skin-to-skin contact with a caregiver, appearing to feel more secure and cry less frequently. Latinos I interviewed confirmed that this is all part of a process of developing a **lifetime responsibility to the family of origin**; other researchers have discovered the same phenomena.

I found that those Latino women who felt that they had failed as mothers left sadness and emptiness in their wake, as though their lives were only half-lived.

The willingness to lose money in order to accommodate the employees' need for a relationship was, for this researcher, a major social statement.

Caregivers stated that infants are rarely put down on the floor or in another place where there is an opportunity to learn to crawl.

High Self-Esteem

Children must not be lost is one of the main goals of Latino women.

I have yet to hear anyone say that domestic obligations are easy enough to allow women time for anything additional, like paid employment. Women are not encouraged to earn an income outside the home. Many men will not allow any work for income, like sewing or baking, to be done in the family home.

Ruth Payne, author of A Framework for Understanding Poverty, describes the poor as *lazy and living in female-centered authoritarian families who are chronically unemployed*. This statement is a gross misrepresentation of my observations of people living in rural Latin America.

People with a continuous income appear to stay in their career/job position until death—that's why their name is embroidered below the logo. Personal power over clients or customers—not over fellow employees—and almost unquestioned authority are the prizes given to people in lieu of a decent salary.

It should be noted that *a large rubber stamp* is a very important status symbol in Latin America. The larger the stamp, the more authority the employee holds within his position of power. The stamp is often used with excessive force when hitting a page—perhaps the loud sound is intended to make the stamp appear larger.

The positive result of the teaching style applied in Latin America was that *a high level of self-discipline was established* within the children. They *learned how to be patient*, to do as they are instructed in a respectful manner, to sit still, and to *encourage and help each other to get the job done*.

It isn't a problem when a Latino is unable to own an item not yet popular, but a commonly used item creates envy among those with- out it and brings status for those who own it. Lacking a popular item ownership due to lack of financial resources is emotionally painful. The difference is in the self-esteem. A wise teacher knows this fact and finds another way to enhance self-esteem.

The list of positive attributes of Latino culture seems endless, and yet not only do educational or intellectual achievements not increase social mobility or social status in Latin America, but such positive efforts just barely improve a person's economic position until at least three consecutive generations have reached the same levels of achievements.

Funds of Knowledge

Educators in the new millennium may have noticed that children seem to lack

1. an identity with place (their community),
2. a play-space knowledge or environmental education (within their schools),
3. a familiarity with their own backyard (classic nature-deficit-disorder) and an overall environmental awareness.

All of life as we know it exists on planet Earth. If we treated our homes or our cars with the same disrespect that we often show for our planet, they would fail far sooner than either our children or our planet might.

Parents and educators need to read the following line before deciding that time in nature is not worth the investment in their children: *The quality of life isn't measured only by what we gain, but also (by) what we trade for it.* Children are suffering from cultural autism by living with tunnel vision. Cultural autism means we are emotionally detached from nature.

Nearly every activity was a family activity *with little in the adult world hidden from small children....Night time does not involve segregation from social life.*

The *campesino* child could be *connecting hand, mind, and community (through) vocational education for social and environmental renewal.*

Spanish Immersion Each One, Teach One

Research, References, and Other Information

The actual meaning of "mordida" offered to a government official in the U.S. would be an illegal bribe. In Latin America, it is actually an anticipated service fee connected with doing business. This service fee applies to any Mexican citizen, in a government office or elsewhere.

Page 152 of the text:

QUESTION 6: "If you were the president of Mexico, what would you do to assure equal educational opportunities for a) children with disabilities, b) rural children, and c) those so poor that at- tending school is an economic hardship for their families?"

REPLY: I would fight corruption and impunity to start with. I would invest more money in education, in order to guarantee that children at risk would really benefit from an education with quality. I would put the union leaders in their place, defending the rights of the teacher, not directing education. I would offer education with quality to adults.

Arizona was one of 38 states misguided into thinking that Dr. Payne I knew what she was taking about regarding the habits of Mexico's poor, who now include my neighbors. I can assure you that her broad derogatory statements related to generational poverty are founded on ignorance about poor subsistence-farming communities in Central and Western Mexico and along the Arizona-Sonora border.

EDUCATORS, take what you will from this workbook. Apply these "tips" in your classroom. Your efforts will create leaders out of Latinos instead of high school dropouts who will live out their adulthood underemployed.

Glossary

Campesino a country person, country dweller, peasant, rural farmer or rancher; frequently the resident is also of indigenous heritage. A Latin American Indian farmer; *campo* is Spanish for *field or country* (Merriam-Webster). All definitions applied to the word *campesino* were used within this research report with the highest degree of respect.

Campo A *campo* is a field, a non-incorporated rural village, pueblo, community, rural residential grouping of people and animals.

Indigenous A person of Native Indian heritage is referred to as of an indigenous culture. Research sites included the following indigenous groups: Guamares, Chichimecas, Guachichile, Otomíes, Purépecha/Tarascan: Celaya, Acámbaro, and Yurirapúndaro. Only the Chichimeca-Jonaz language is still used (Schmal, n.d.).

Developmental Delay A diagnosis of developmental delay typically occurs when a child has failed to meet a predictable milestone or more than one milestone relative to their cultural standards. Identifying if this failure might have a long-term affect on a child's speech and language, fine and gross motor skills, and/or personal and social skills an intervention is normally advised (ERIC, 1999).

The Relationship Factor This phrase is used in scholarly papers to explain personal interactions between people (Spence et al., 2002). This book uses this phrase to explain the primary force observed to be of the utmost importance in Mexican communities: caring for and personal histories with others, including family, extended family, and friends. In Mexico, relationships are held of higher importance than money, employment, status, power, position, or any other distraction requiring time, energy, or other resources (Ogbu, 1992b; Rogoff, 2003; Valdés, 1996; Valenzuela, 1999). The Mexican culture deifies ancestors (Mackenzie, 2008); all domestic duties, income-producing responsibilities, and other roles must be referred to with great caution and extreme cultural sensitivity (Saracho & Martinez-Hancock, 2004), because saving face and preserving pride are of paramount value (Mackenzie, 2009; Valdés, 1996). Passing a person on the street or in a public bathroom requires asking permission of the other person: *"Con permiso"* (with your permission). Entering a doctor's office or another public space requires everyone in the room to receive a general greeting and eye contact: *"Buenos dias"*/*"Buenos tardes"*/*"Buenos noches"* (good day/good afternoon/good night) (Valdés, 1996). People of all ages will respond automatically when greeted in this manner using the same greeting. A greeting is initiated anytime a person enters a room or comes within a distance of 20 feet, even outdoors in undefined spaces. There is often a shortage of economic resources in Mexico, but there is no shortage of respect and an acknowledgement of respect for interdependence and its sociocultural influence (Ogbu, 1992b; Rogoff, 2003; Valdés, 1996; Valenzuela, 1999; Velez-Ibanez, 1992; Zembylas, 2002).

Other Books by the Author

Empowering Spanish Speakers—Answers for Educators, Business People, and Friends of Latinos

Sociocultural Influences: Evaluations of Indigenous Children for Special Needs in Rural Central Mexico

Victoria's Crown

Thank You—Gracias

Net proceeds from the sale of this book help to support our non-profit programs.

This book earns money support teaching English, providing equine therapy and water therapy to disabled people, making swimming opportunities available for rural children, to build libraries in rural Mexico and to preserve their lifestyle through written records while increasing their opportunities to grow mentally and economically. These Native Indians have always been oppressed. Statistics tell us that they are the most likely to run to the north border. With access to knowledge they can remain in Mexico, remain with their families, and keep their indigenous roots. Thank you for helping to reduce emigration.

About the Author

DR. JACQUELINE ZALESKI MACKENZIE is the first academic researcher to relocate permanently to a low-socioeconomic-status village in rural Central Mexico. She is an expert in the education of Mexicans and management of nonprofit corporations. She was an Arizona-certified teacher with over 95% Mexican students and has taught in Mexico beginning May 2005. Her doctoral award from the University of Arizona included exceptional education, bilingual education and sociocultural studies, including four research projects in Mexico. Since 1986, she has continuously served as a nonprofit administrator, using skills acquired from her formal education in Business Systems Management and expertise acquired from over 40 years of business management work. She holds Master of Science and Bachelor of Science degrees from Florida Institute of Technology. Her faith, compassion, and passion for fairness also led her to earn a Bachelor of Arts in Divinity from Universal Brotherhood. Her spirit of adventure was nurtured in a military family, with father, uncle, and husband serving in the U.S. Air Force, and son serving in the U.S. Army. Her father served under General Curtis E. LeMay; he was once transferred 22 times in 22 months. Her playmates came from diverse cultures. Inspiration from family military history—which includes relatives serving in World War II, Korean War, and Vietnam—led her to become an FAA-certified flight instructor; she was the only pilot flying a round trip from Florida to Alaska and back to Florida. (In Alaska, she met fellow trailblazer Astronaut Sally Ride and visited an Inuit village.) A feminist, she was the first female Teamster in Chicago (second in U.S.) and belonged to the initial group of women

63

to pass the Illinois State Trooper's Exam. Her dedication to ecology began in high school; her residence for 12 years (1996–2008) was off the power grid on the Arizona/Sonora border. Her imagination led her to study Art Education for six quarters at the University of Illinois Circle Campus and for two years under the late artist/sculptor Robert Von Neumann. Her astrological birth chart shows that her sun, moon, and Mercury are placed within 2 degrees of each other in the sign of Aquarius: She is an idealist, a reformer, and a rebel with Virgo rising, which also makes her service-oriented. Her Myers-Briggs personality type is ENTJ, representative of an assertive, innovative, long-range thinker with an excellent ability to adapt theories and possibilities into concrete plans of action.

Dr. Mackenzie was awarded the Able Toastmaster Silver distinction. She is a charismatic and inspirational speaker. She won a Toastmasters Regional Award for her public speaking after completing 350 presentations in 24 months. As a professional student, she welcomes readers' feedback.

Contact her at: jzm@email.arizona.edu

or:

220 North Zapata Hwy, Suite 11
PMB 512-A
Laredo, TX 78043-4464

www.jacquelinemackenzie.com
www.spanishimmersioneducation.org